Tanaka Grant Publishing House,
2016

It was just them that day, the owl and the moon, for the owl's date the sun had already sang its tune.

So it had set, and the moon had risen, the owl's white coat went from a yellow to a soft crimson.

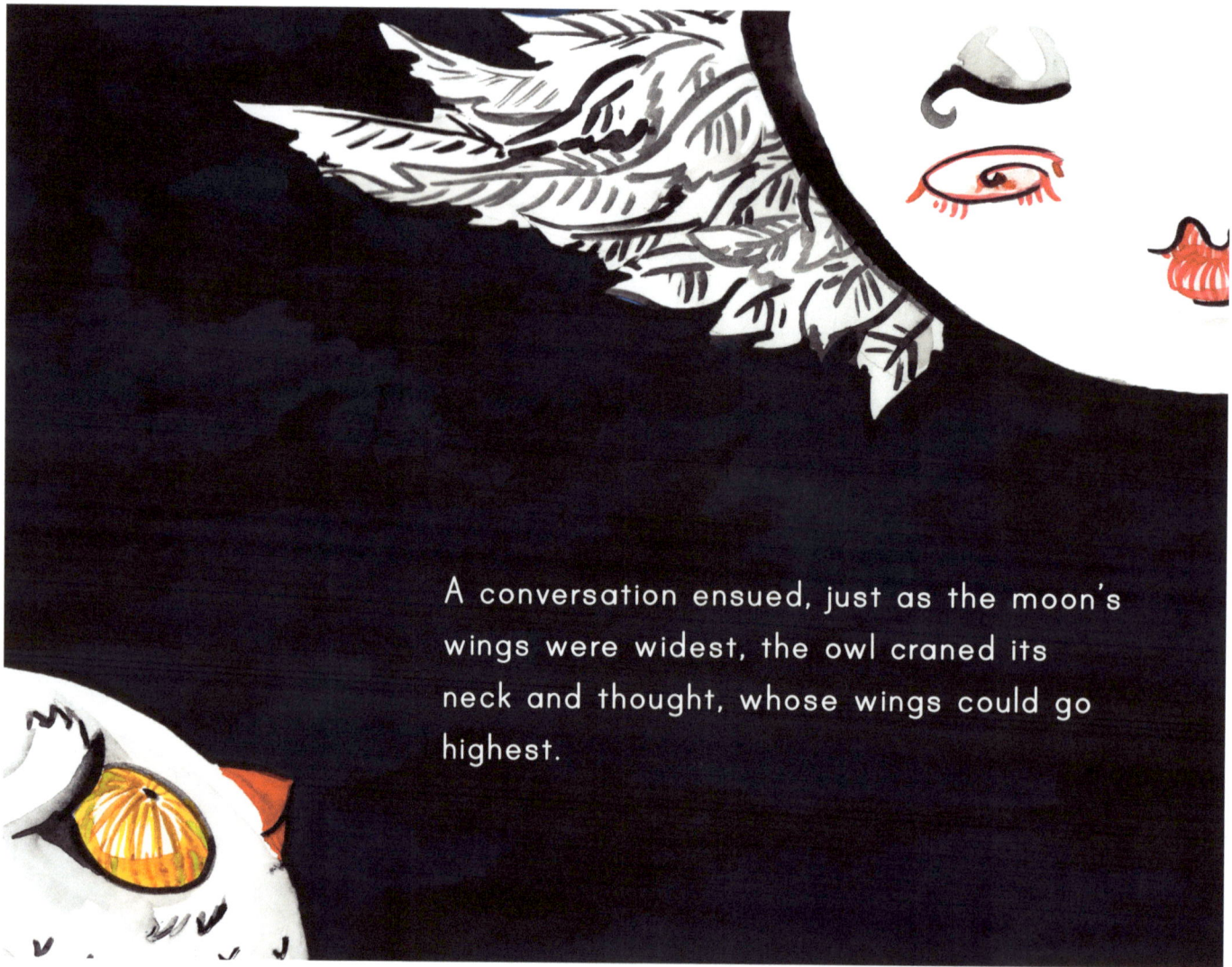

A conversation ensued, just as the moon's wings were widest, the owl craned its neck and thought, whose wings could go highest.

"Look at these!"
The owl said,
nearly falling off
the tree.

"I said look at
these!" The owl
yelled again,
arms in full flex.

But the moon said
nothing, in spite of
the childish plea.

4

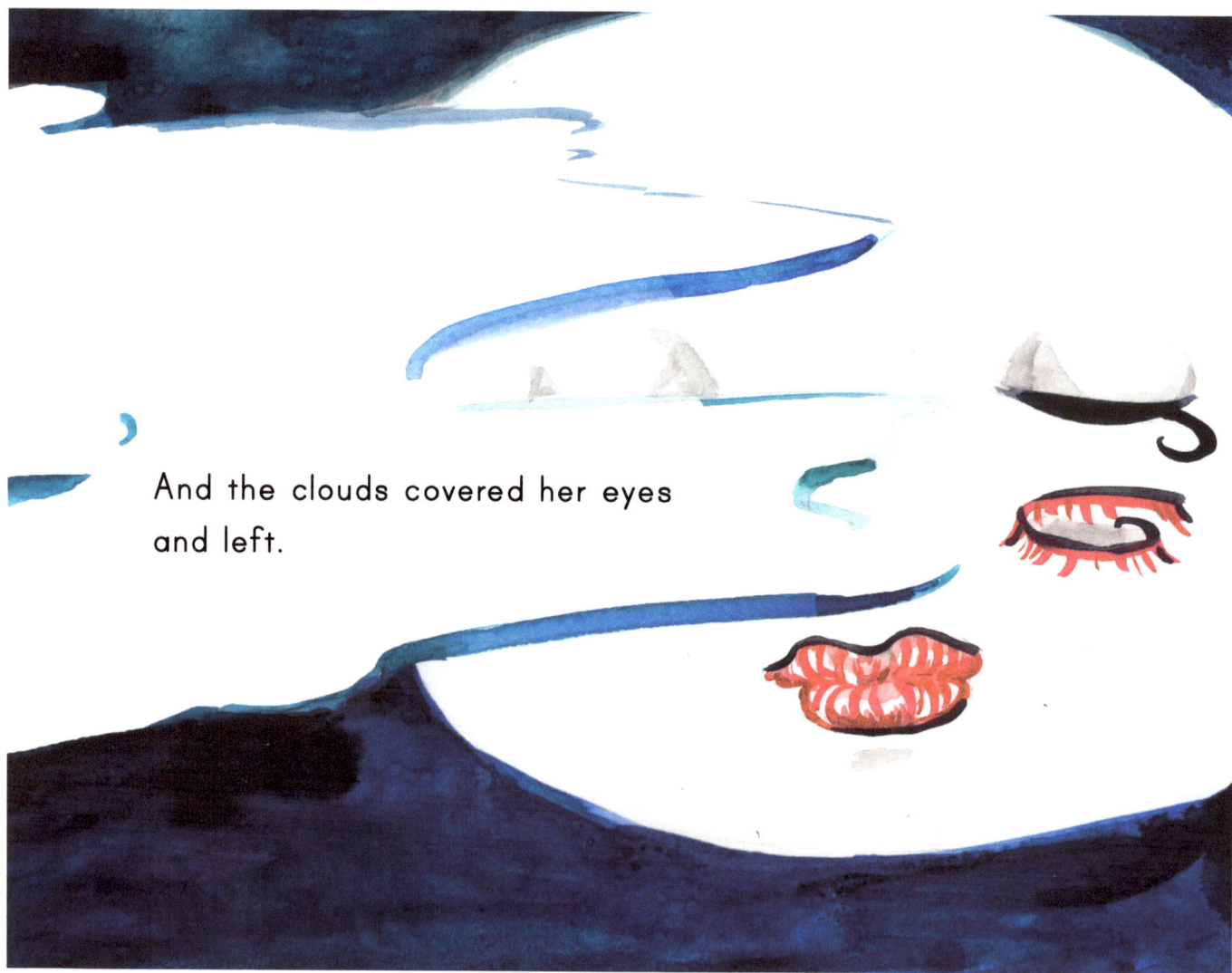

And the clouds covered her eyes
and left.

The owl looked around

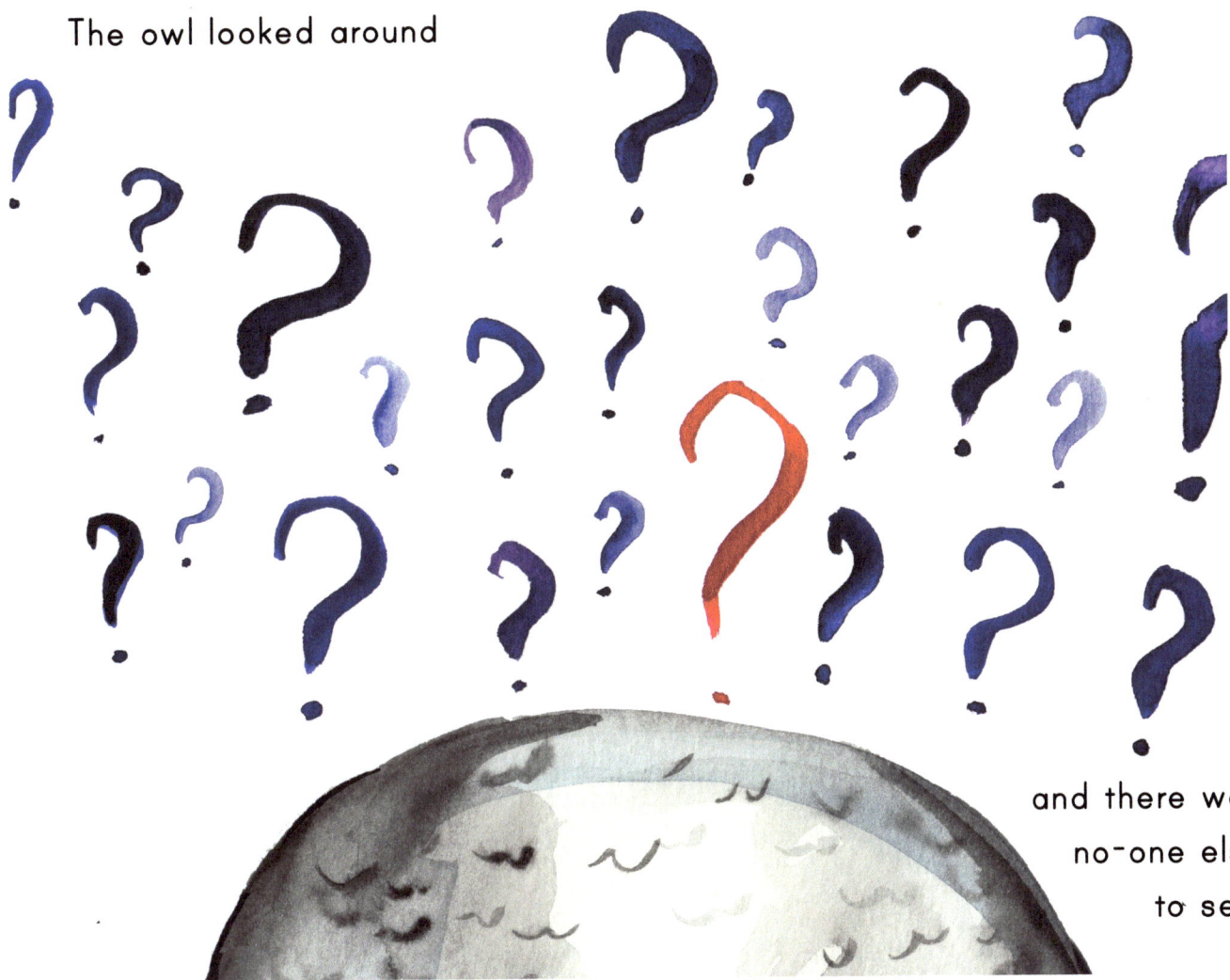

and there was
no-one else
to see.

6

"Hello up there! G'day!"

"What is it that you be?"

The owl went on...

Won't you come down from
there for a hot cup of

And still the moon said
nothing in spite of the owl's
plea.

The owl sighed, he let out a

hmpf...

The branch
beneath him
swayed and he
was now quiet.

12

A star flickered just as
he went silent.

So the owl was glowing and the
moon didn't hoot, the clouds
were clearing and the stars didn't
shoot

The wind didn't blow,
the streetlights they just
flashed, and the owl's
thoughts had up and passed.

The owl now knew
the moon wouldn't
answer

So he perched and
closed his eyes,
knowing the sun
would up and rise,
and he said nothing,
and so heard
everything, as the
moon just waned
and smiled.

It was just them that day, the owl and the moon, and the owl's date the sun was ready to sing its tune.

The owl would not speak
until the sun had fully risen

He learned this from the moon, and its white and silent decision.

Story By Alexander Grant,
Illustrated by Lindsay Tanaka

A Note on the Author and Illustrator

Alexander Grant knew an owl once, and knew it well,
and hopes that this story explains that and explains
it well. Lindsay Tanaka is already known by another
name, in another life, another land where she shares
her tea with the pale-faced moon.

www.ingramcontent.com/pod-product-compliance
Lightning Source LLC
Chambersburg PA
CBHW042021090426
42811CB00016B/1700